MY FISH

Me and My PET

By William Anthony

BookLife
PUBLISHING

©2019
BookLife Publishing Ltd.
King's Lynn
Norfolk PE30 4LS

A catalogue record for this book is available from the British Library.

ISBN: 978-1-78637-577-3

Written by:
William Anthony

Edited by:
Robin Twiddy

Designed by:
Jasmine Pointer

Photocredits:

Images are courtesy of Shutterstock.com. With thanks to Getty Images, Thinkstock Photo and iStockphoto.

Front cover - Max Topchii, Igor Kovalchuk. 2 - Green Jo. 3 - Alena Ohneva, Teerapong Jirojkul. 4 - Max Topchii. 5 - Teerapong Jirojkul. 6 - Jovan Barajevac. 7 - hedgehog94. 8 - Frantisek Czanner. 9 - Dobermaraner. 10 - satit_srihin. 11 - Tretyakov Viktor. 12 - Monika Wisniewska. 13 - Sergei Kolesnikov. 14 - Andrey Armyagov. 15 - val lawless. 18 - You Touch Pix of EuToch. 17 - Suchart Boonyavech. 18 - Max Topchii. 19 - Martin Carlsson. 20 - topimages. 21 - Grigorev Mikhai. 22 - Max Topchii. 23 - ANURAK PONGPATIMET.

CONTENTS

Words that look like this can be found in the glossary on page 24.

Nigel ♥ and Chips

Hello! My name's Nigel, and this is my pet fish, Chips. He's five years old. Fish are my favourite animal because they're very colourful and fun to watch.

Nigel →

Chips

Whether you're thinking about keeping fish, or you already have some, Chips and I are going to take you through how to look after your pet fish!

Lead the way, Chips!

Getting a Fish

Getting fish and looking after them means you are going to have a lot of **responsibility**. You will need to feed them, and give them a nice home with lots of places to explore.

Always check which fish can be kept together before you buy new ones!

My family got Chips from a pet shop. He is a fighting fish, which means he needs to be kept alone. Lots of other types of fish like to be kept in large groups.

Home

Fish need to be kept in a special type of tank called an aquarium (say: ak-wear-ee-um). Aquariums stop water from escaping and keep it at the right temperature.

Fish need to be kept in the right kind of water. Marine fish like salt water. Tropical fish like warm, fresh water, while other fish like it cold.

You can keep the water clean with a filter, and keep it warm with a heater.

Playtime

Fish aren't like other pets. Most other pets can be stroked or cuddled, but fish need to stay in water all the time.

Fish can't breathe out of water, so don't take them out of it!

Fish are still fun pets to keep though, and you can **design** their aquarium any way you like! You can put in lots of **ornaments** and plants to make their tank look exciting!

Food

Flake Food

Fish are very easy to feed. They eat flakes and wafers of food. You can buy this from a pet shop.

12

You need to feed your fish either once or twice a day.
All you need to do is drop in a pinch of food.
It should be just enough to be eaten after five minutes.

13

Bedtime ^zᶻᶻ

Lots of people think fish don't sleep because they don't lie down or close their eyes. However, even though it is different to how humans do it, fish do sleep.

Fish can sleep at any time of the day or night, but you won't know they are asleep. This is because fish don't have eyelids, so it's very hard to tell!

The Vet

Vets are like doctors, but for animals instead of humans.

Fish can get ill, just like humans. Fish that are ill can go to the vets. The vet will do everything they can to help your fish get better again.

One day when I came home,
Chips had some white spots.
I told my parents and we took
him to a vet that treats fish.
The vet made him all
better again.

If you think your fish
isn't very well, make sure
you tell someone.

17

Growing Up

This fish has lost its really bright red colour!

Chips is quite old for a fighting fish. They live for between five and seven years. Some fish might start to lose their colours or get quite thin when they're old.

Cleaning your aquarium **regularly** will help your fish live to a good age.

Super Fish

WOW!

All fish are different, but some fish are simply super! Puffer fish are marine fish. Some people have seen them do tricks such as swimming backwards when they want food!

There is a type of tropical fish called a glass fish. They're called glass fish because they are **transparent** like glass! You can see their skeletons as they swim around.

You ♥ and Your Pet

Whichever type of fish you have, make sure you take care of them, just like Chips and I have shown you.

I'm sure you'll make a great pet owner. Try to think of a cool **theme** for your tank; you might choose a pirate shipwreck, a castle, or something else. Most importantly, have fun with your new fishy friends!

GLOSSARY

design	to plan and make decisions about how a thing will be made
ornaments	things used for decoration
regularly	at the same time every day, week, month or year
responsibility	having tasks that you are expected to do
temperature	how hot or cold something is
theme	a style or set of ideas something is based on
transparent	see-through
tropical	hot and humid

INDEX